NIKKI YANOFSKY

NIKKI

ISBN 978-1-4234-9889-6

HAL•LEONARD®
CORPORATION
7777 W. BLUEMOUND RD. P.O. BOX 13819 MILWAUKEE, WI 53213

Visit Hal Leonard Online at
www.halleonard.com

TAKE THE "A" TRAIN

Words and Music by
BILLY STRAYHORN

Fast Swing, with a groove

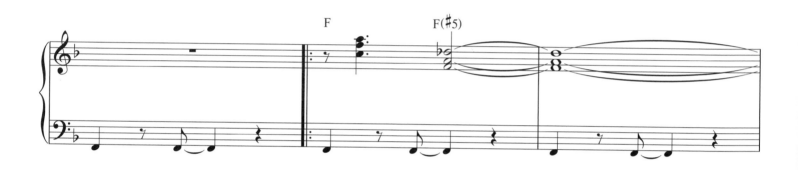

NEVER MAKE IT ON TIME

Words and Music by NICOLE YANOFSKY,
JESSE HARRIS and RON SEXSMITH

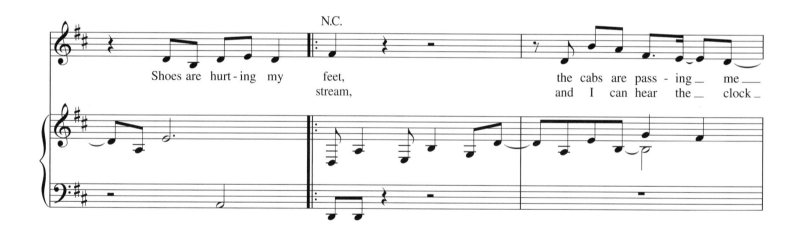

Shoes are hurt-ing my feet,
stream,

the cabs are pass-ing me
and I can hear the clock

by.
chime.

I'm tak-ing all the wrong streets,
Feels like I'm in a bad dream,

I'll nev-er make it on time.
I'll nev-er make it on time. I'll nev-er make it on

time, I'm ___ try'n' ___ to get to you, some-thing ___ just ___

___ won't ___ let me through. I don't know what ___ I'm gon-na do,

help me ___ please. ___

Feels like I'm swim-ming up -

I GOT RHYTHM

Music and Lyrics by GEORGE GERSHWIN
and IRA GERSHWIN

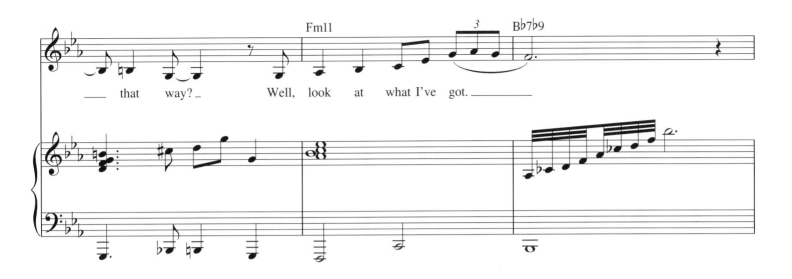

Fm11   Bb7b9

that way? _ Well, look at what I've got. _____

Fast Swing

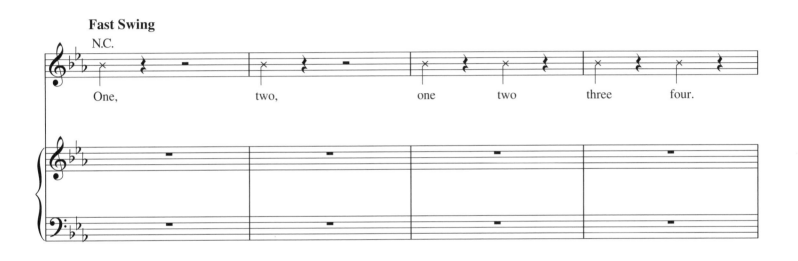

N.C.

One, two, one two three four.

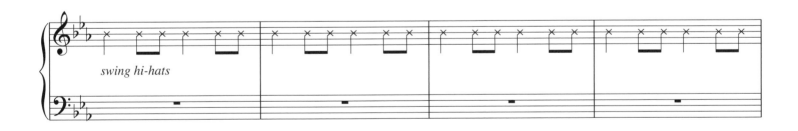

swing hi-hats

Bbdim7   Bb7b9

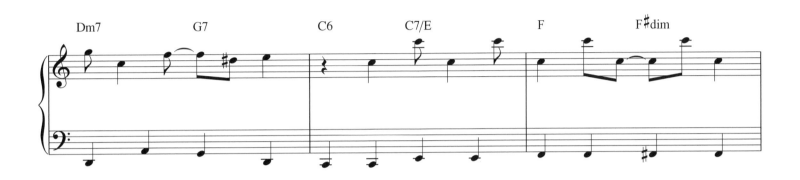

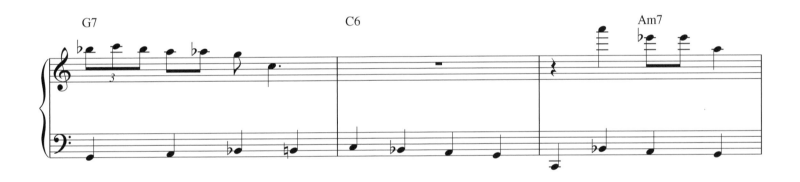

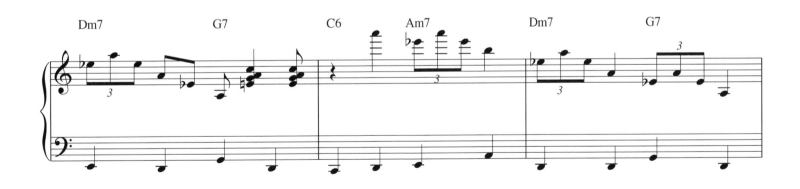

G6

I want to be hap - py, but I won't be ___ hap - py

'til I make you ___ hap - py too.

Bb6

Life won't be worth liv - ing if we are both giv - ing,

D.S. al Coda

Eb6

I will give ___ some to you, yeah.

FOR ANOTHER DAY

Words and Music by NICOLE YANOFSKY,
JESSE HARRIS and RON SEXSMITH

Slowly, with movement

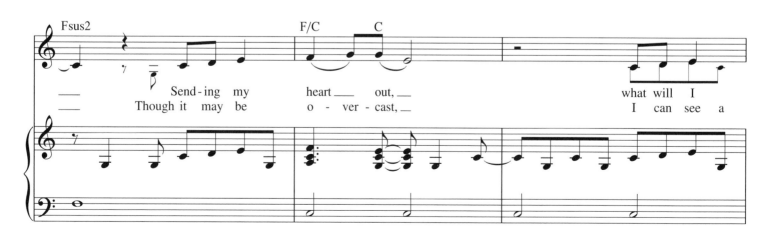

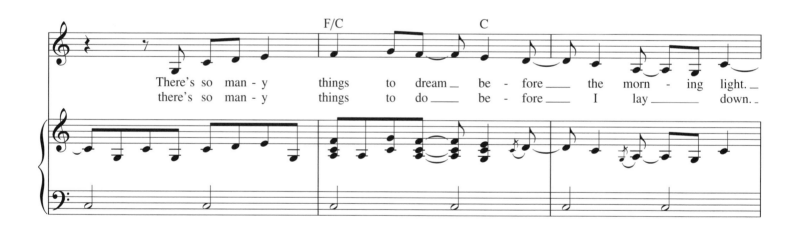

28

And don't it seem strange how — dreams just float __ a - way? _____

time just drifts _ a - way? _____

GOD BLESS' THE CHILD

Words and Music by ARTHUR HERZOG JR.
and BILLIE HOLIDAY

To Coda ⊕

own.

Oh, mon - ey,

you've got lots of friends, they're crowd - ing 'round your door.

COOL MY HEELS

Words and Music by NICOLE YANOFSKY,
JESSE HARRIS and RON SEXSMITH

Moderate groove

(1., D.S.) Cool ____ my heels ____ when ____ the heat ____ is on. ____
(2.) Cool ____ my heels ____ be - fore ____ I lose ____ con - trol. ____

Slow ____ my wheels ____ when ____ it feels all wrong. ____
This dev - il deal ____ is 'bout ____ to take my soul. ____

IF YOU CAN'T SING IT
(You'll Have to Swing It)
from the Paramount Picture RHYTHM ON THE RANGE

Words and Music by
SAM COSLOW

The con - cert was o - ver in Car - ne - gie hall; the
maes - tro took bow af - ter bow. He said, "My dear friends, I have
giv - en my all. I'm sor - ry; it's all o - ver now,"

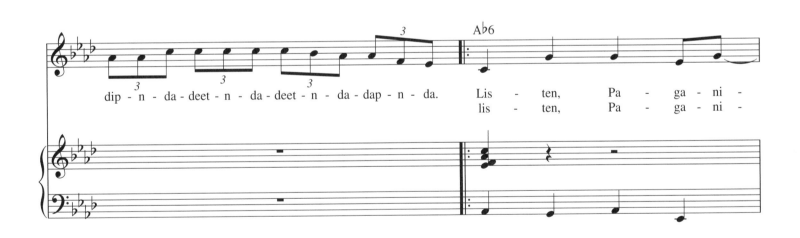

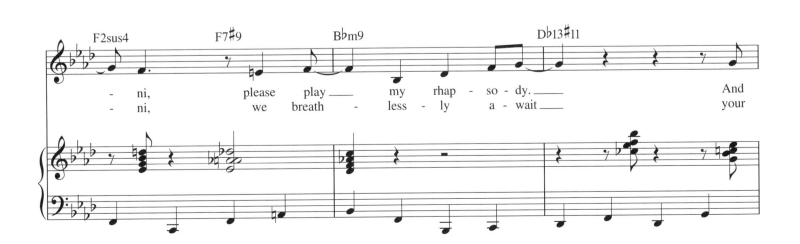

BIENVENUE DANS MA VIE

Words and Music by NICOLE YANOFSKY,
JESSE HARRIS and RON SEXSMITH

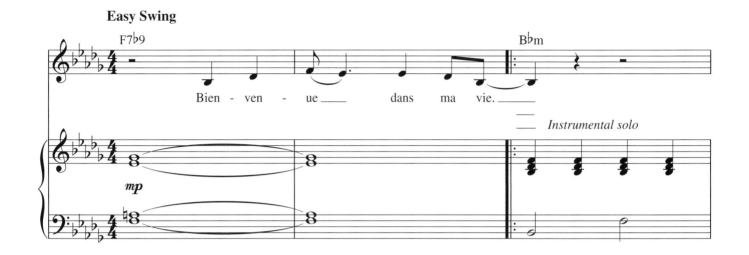

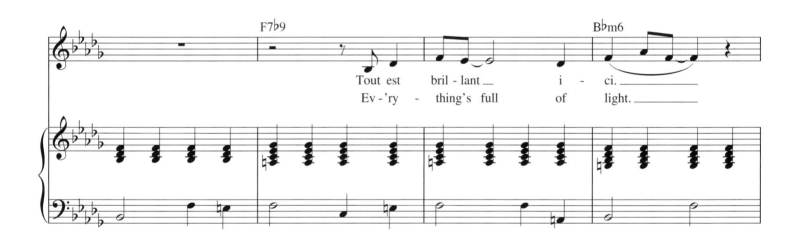

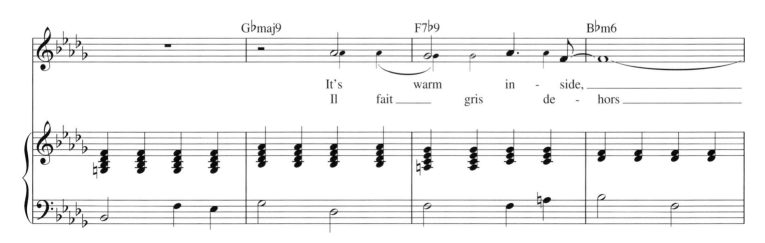

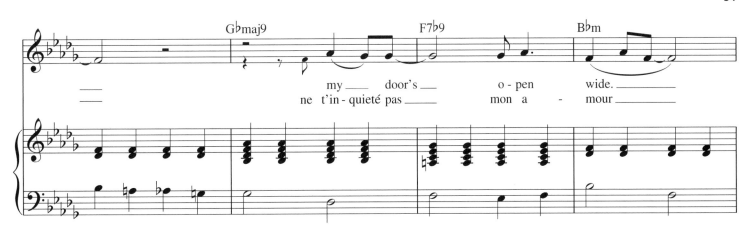

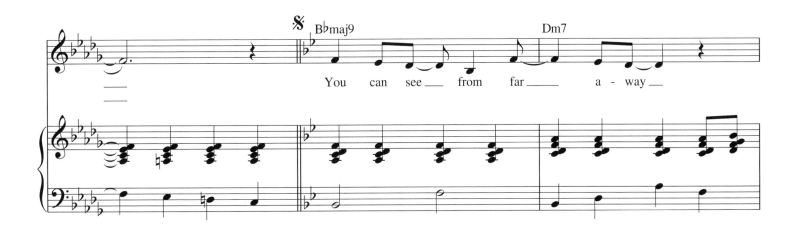

for - get your strife. _____

There's a light ___ on in ___ the hall, ___ lead - ing to ___ a place ___

where you can fall ___ and rest your ___ head. ___ Close ___ your eyes, ___

To Coda ⊕

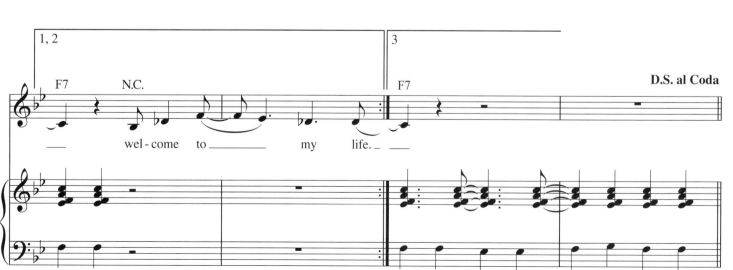

1, 2

3

D.S. al Coda

___ wel - come to _____ my life. ___

CODA

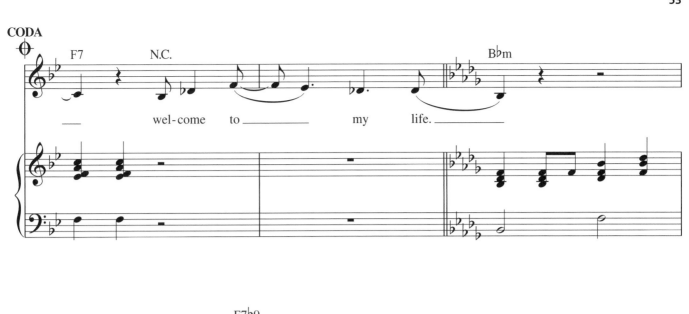

wel-come to _____ my life. ____

Wel-come to _____ my _____ life. __

Do ba do do do do do do, bien-ven -

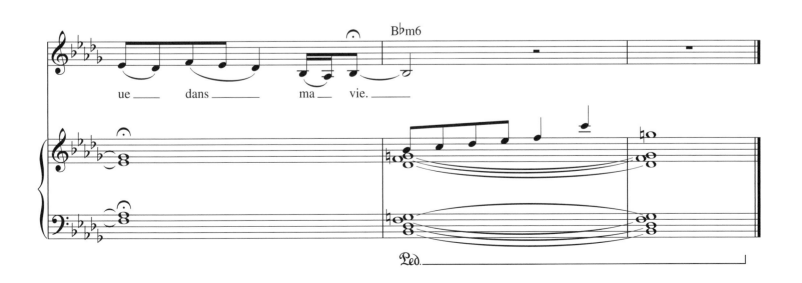

ue ____ dans _____ ma __ vie. ____

FIRST LADY

Words and Music by NICOLE YANOFSKY
and ROBI BOTOS

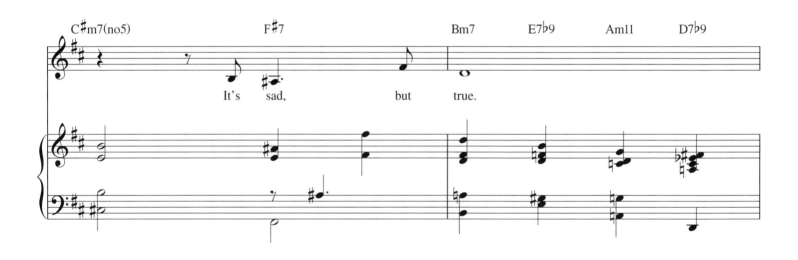

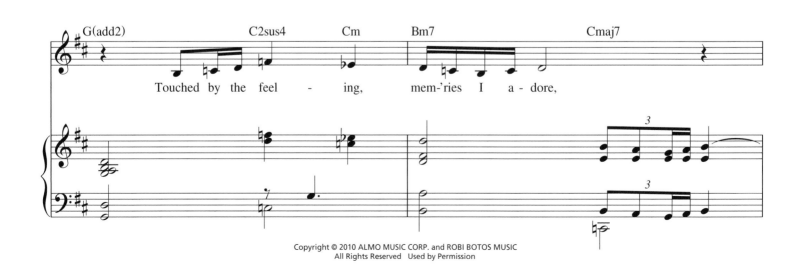

ON THE SUNNY SIDE OF THE STREET/ FOOL IN THE RAIN

Half-time Shuffle

FOOL IN THE RAIN
Music and Lyrics by JOHN PAUL JONES,
JIMMY PAGE and ROBERT PLANT

Ooh, oh.

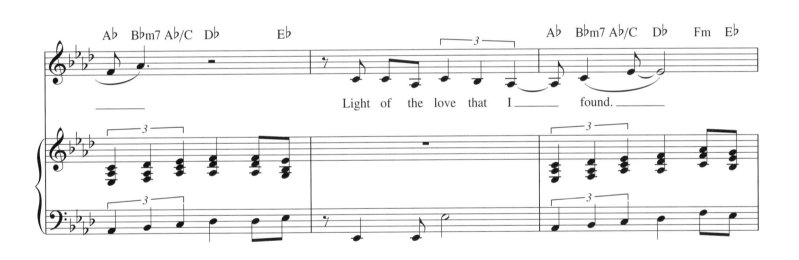

Light of the love that I found.

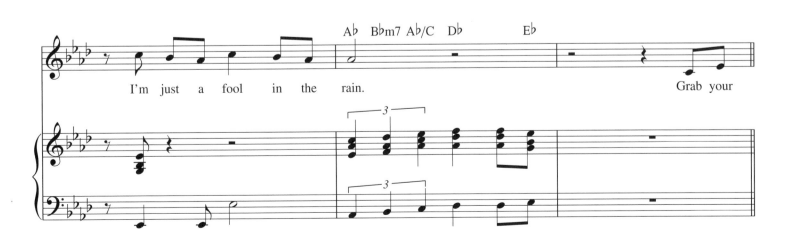

I'm just a fool in the rain. Grab your

ON THE SUNNY SIDE OF THE STREET
Lyric by DOROTHY FIELDS
Music by JIMMY McHUGH

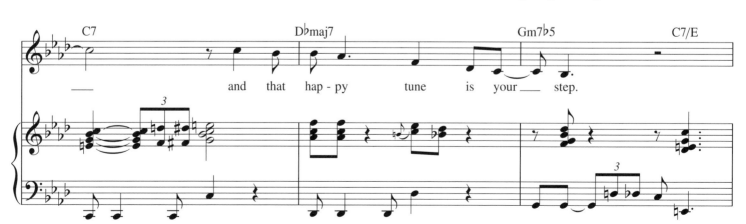

60

GREY SKIES

Words and Music by NICOLE YANOFSKY,
SHARADA BANMAN and PAUL SHROFEL

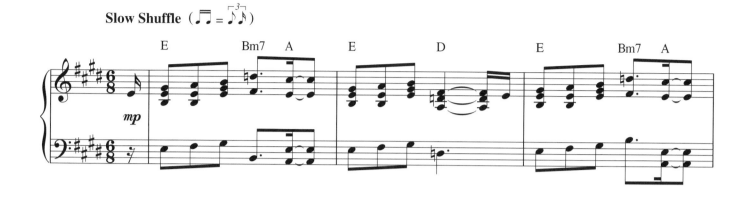

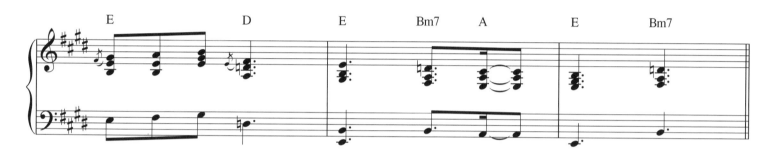

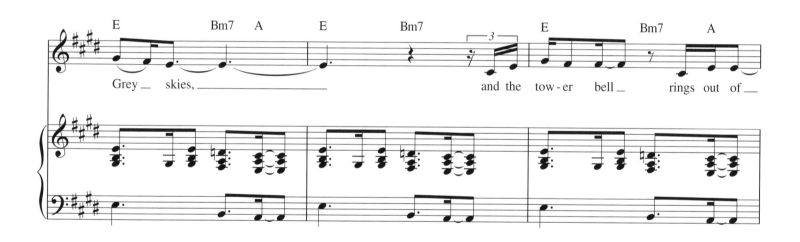

Grey _ skies, _____ and the tow-er bell _ rings out of _

_ time. Week days are roll-ing by, all while the de-mons cry. _

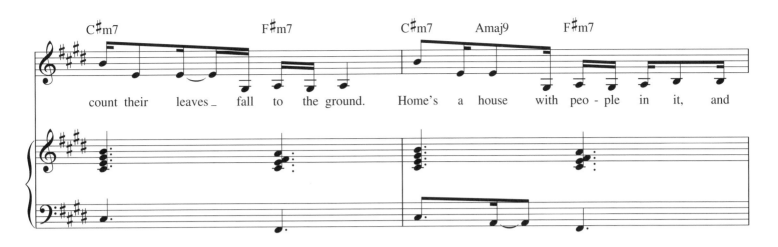

TRY TRY TRY

Words and Music by
LESLIE FEIST

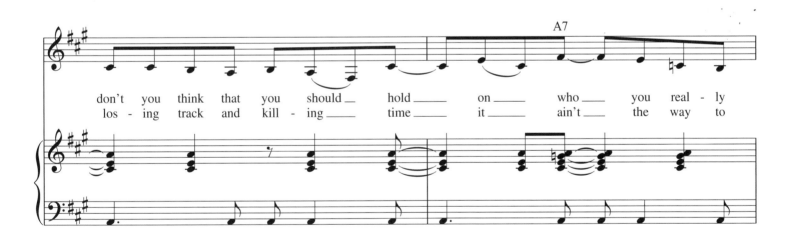

OVER THE RAINBOW
from THE WIZARD OF OZ

Music by HAROLD ARLEN
Lyric by E.Y. "YIP" HARBURG

AIR MAIL SPECIAL

Music by BENNY GOODMAN,
JIMMY MUNDY and CHARLIE CHRISTIAN

Fast Swing

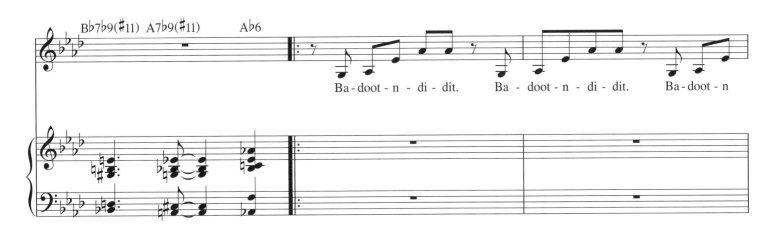

Ba - doot - n - di - dit.   Ba - doot - n - di - dit.   Ba - doot - n

did - dl - y - um,   did - dl - y - um,   dit - di - dee. ___   Ba - doot - n - di - dit.   Ba -

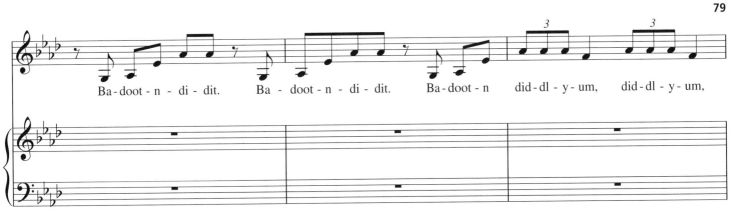

Ba - doot - n - di - dit. Ba - doot - n - di - dit. Ba - doot - n did - dl - y - um, did - dl - y - um,

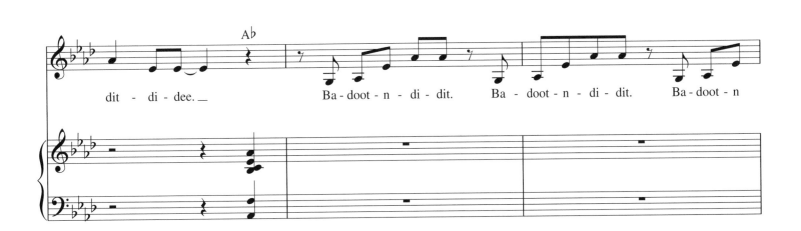

dit - di - dee.___ Ba - doot - n - di - dit. Ba - doot - n - di - dit. Ba - doot - n

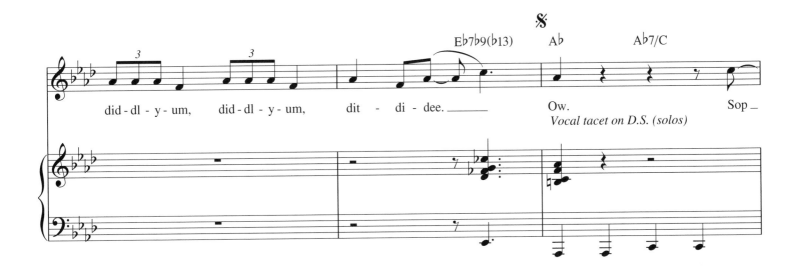

did - dl - y - um, did - dl - y - um, dit - di - dee._____ Ow. Sop ___

Vocal tacet on D.S. (solos)

___ bop bop ___ bop be do dow. Stip - py dip - py dip ba dip - n

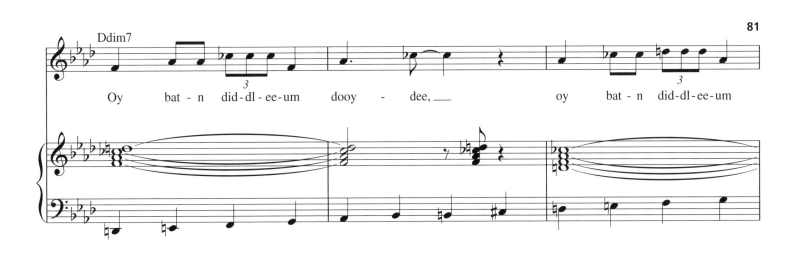

Oy bat - n did - dl - ee-um dooy - dee, _____ oy bat - n did-dl-ee-um

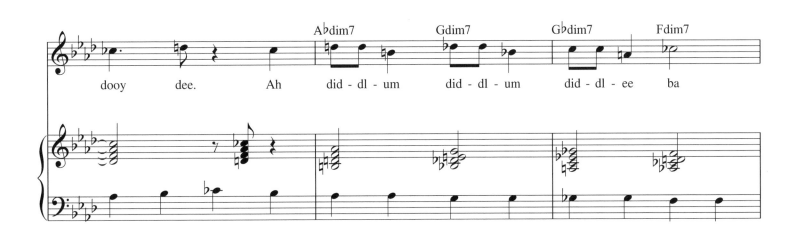

dooy dee. Ah did - dl - um did - dl - um did - dl - ee ba

seb ah de be de ba de ba de ba de ba da. _____ ba - dip - n doo - dee,

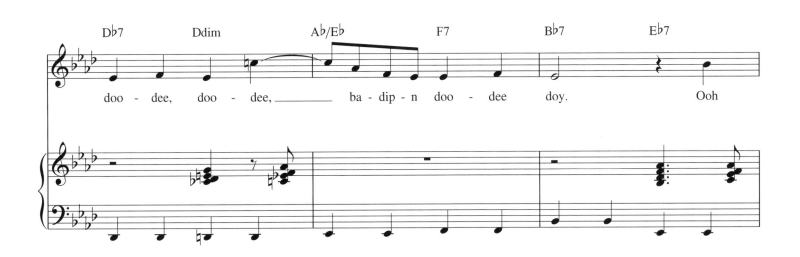

doo - dee, doo - dee, _____ ba - dip - n doo - dee doy. Ooh

To Coda

doop - a - dip, doo - dee, doo - dee, doo - deep - a - dip - n doo - dee

doy. Zip - a - dee doo - day, doy - deep bah,

ba - ba - doo - bee - ow, beep, bap, beep, ba. Dav - ey,

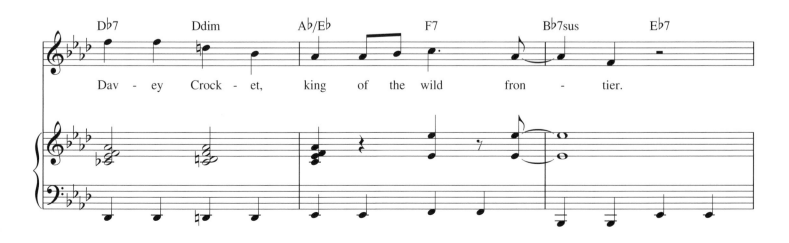

Dav - ey Crock - et, king of the wild fron - tier.

84

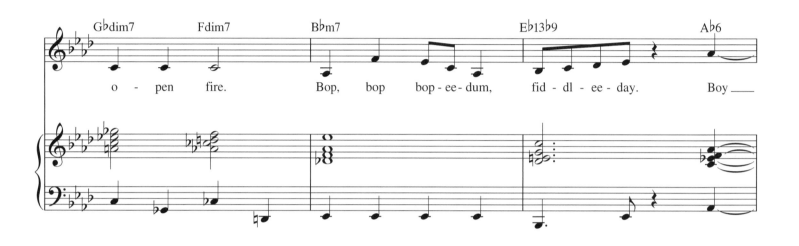

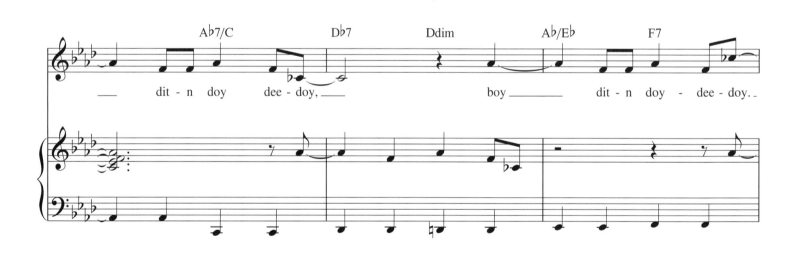

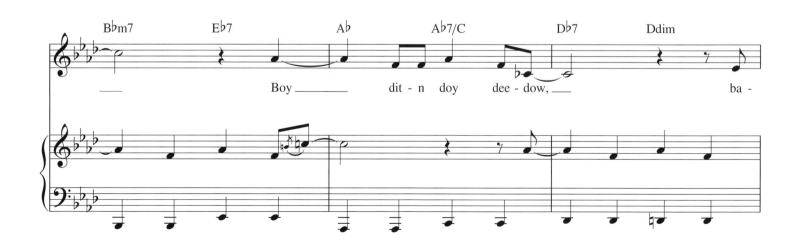

89

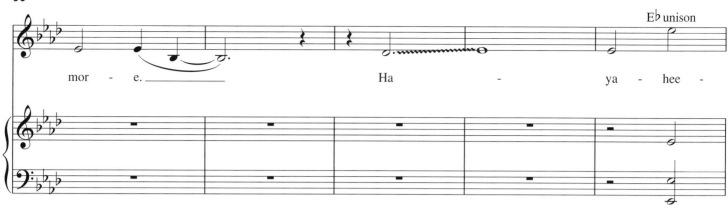

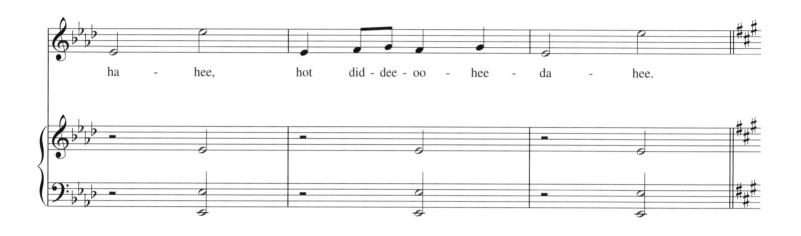

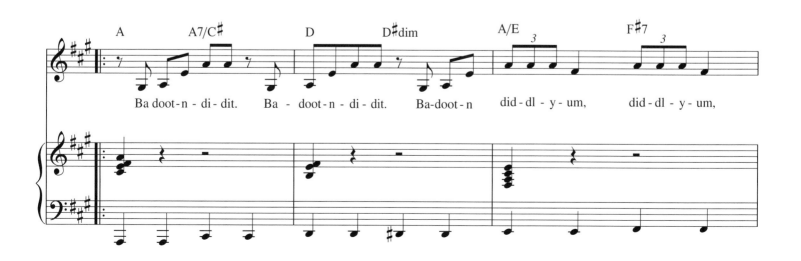

I BELIEVE
Vancouver 2010 CTV Olympic Theme Song

Words and Music by STEPHAN MOCCIO
and ALAN FREW

Moderately

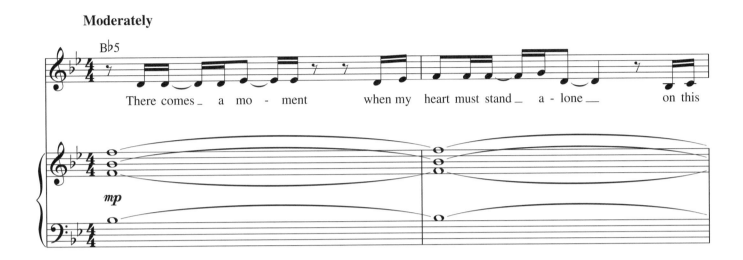

There comes _ a mo - ment when my heart must stand _ a - lone _ on this

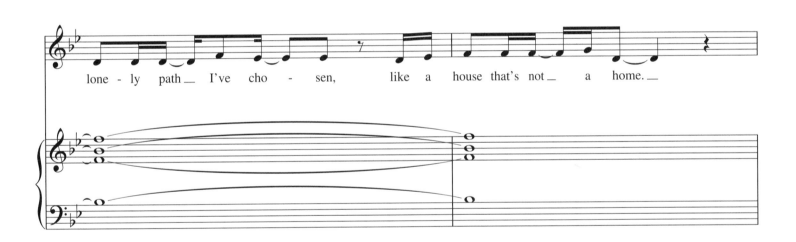

lone - ly path _ I've cho - sen, like a house that's not _ a home. _

Some - times _ when I feel I've had e - nough, _ and I feel _ like giv - ing

O CANADA!

By CALIXA LAVALLEE,
l'HON. JUDGE ROUTHIER
and JUSTICE R.S. WEIR

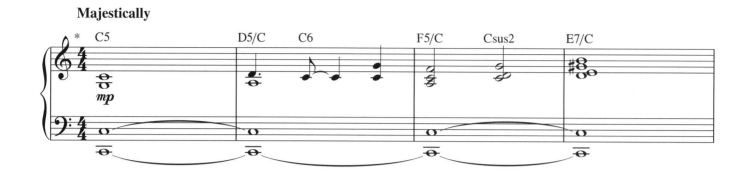

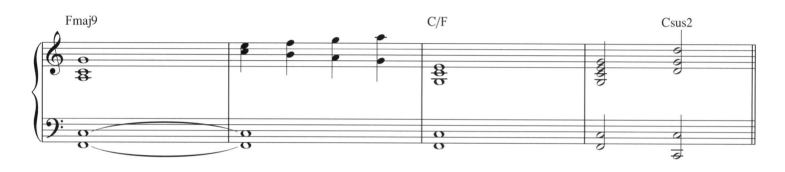

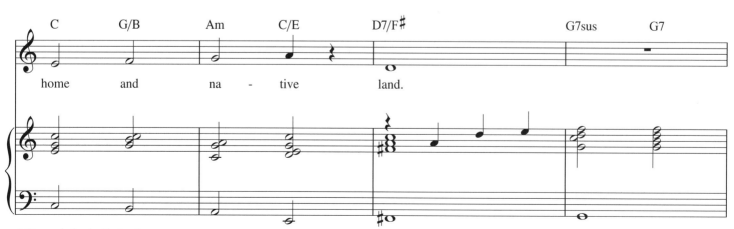

Recorded a half-step lower

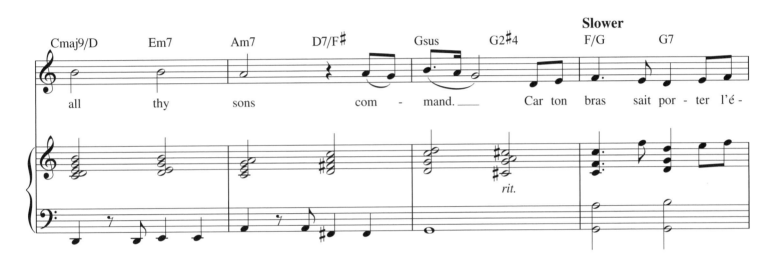

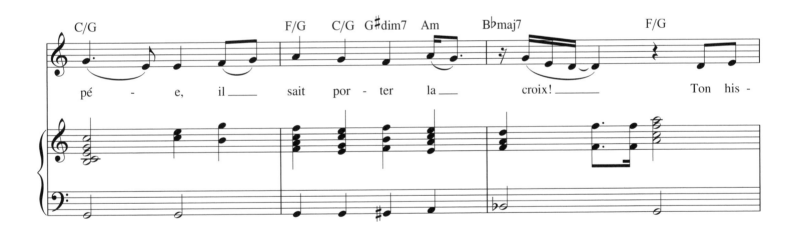